MOST
EMBARRASSING
MOMENTS...

The Book of
CRINGE

First published in Great Britain in 2005
by Artnik
341b Queenstown Road
London SW8 4LH
UK

© Artnik 2005

ISBN 1-903906-52-0

Design: Supriya Sahai
Research: Kostas Savalas and Barrie Creamer

Printed in Spain by Gráficas Díaz

MOST
EMBARRASSING
MOMENTS...

The Book of
CRINGE

artnik books

Cringe is the emotion of social death.

Cringe is pop culture's new Frankenstein monster, and it's bigger than horror ever was. It's the aesthetic of *The Office* and reality TV: people making exhibitions of themselves in the way that the presentation of themselves to others is undermined, stripped or is so incompetent that they are exposed as pathetic, inadequate and, most of all, embarrassing.

Everyone has their own cringe memories that, however long ago they occurred, still make them want to curl up and die. To be severely embarrassed is to lose one's social identity, to lose one's sense of worth, it is to lose face. Consequently the emotion of cringe physically mimics shrinking away from the world. It's power is reflected in how the intensity of the memory rarely fades over time. Cringe is as basic to the human condition as guilt.

Most Embarrassing moments... is a collection of other people's cringes as recalled by the famous, infamous, ordinary and anonymous.

By the way, relishing other people's cringe makes your own more bearable.

John McVicar

Beverley Knight

It still makes me tingle, remembering it.
It was a production of *Joseph and his
Amazing Technicolour Dreamcoat*. I was
the narrator, the biggest singing part. I'm
very short-sighted, and I was 15 and
really vain, and I didn't want to wear
glasses on stage. I had to appear at the
top of the stairs constructed on stage and
walk down them singing. The house lights
go on and I go to put my foot on the
stairs and I stood on my trousers. I was
too blind to see and put my other foot out
and slipped all the way down the stairs.

The whole school was there. I was in the
fifth year and all the first years were at
the front watching. They howled! I still
stood up and sang. The shame would have
killed me otherwise. The trouble was the
fall had knocked out my voice. All I could
do was croak.
It was the end.

One-Night-Stand Shocker

I was at a party with a bunch of my friends when I bumped into Chris, a guy I'd had a crush on since high school but hadn't seen in years. We ended up talking for most of the night, but after we'd had a few drinks, he excused himself to go to the bathroom. When I bumped into him a few minutes later, I suggested that he come home with me. He seemed a little confused at first, but we ended up having an amazing night.

The next morning, I woke up with the worst hangover I'd ever had; I rolled over and said, 'Chris, that was the best.' He looked oddly shamefaced. Then, he said quietly, 'I'm not Chris, I'm his twin Mike.'

I'd slept with someone I didn't even know!

Diss-Connected

I was having lunch with my friend Sara when my cell phone rang. When I checked the number and saw that it was Scott, a guy I'd slept with a few weeks before, I shut off the ringer and rolled my eyes.

Sara asked what was wrong, so I told her how bad he was in bed and started **wagging my limp French fry** to describe his penis.

We both started cracking up, but all of a sudden, Sara kicked my leg hard under the table. I turned around and almost died; Scott was standing right behind my chair with a cell phone in his hand.

[Fact: 40% HAVE BEEN CAUGHT BY AN EX WHILE TRASHING THEM BEHIND – OR SO THEY THOUGHT – THEIR BACK.]

Dirty-Letter Lolita

I was babysitting, and while the kids were napping, I decided to sit at their desk and write a note to my boyfriend, Brian. I made it really racy and described in detail how I wanted to go down on him the next time we could sneak into his shower together. I was folding up the note when one of the kids started screaming, so I dropped everything and ran inside.

The next day, the woman I'd babysat for came to my house. She said she was appalled that I thought her husband would ever want to be with me and handed me the note she said she'd found on her desk. I explained that it was for my boyfriend Brian, but before I could say anything else, she narrowed her eyes and said,

'My husband is not your boyfriend.'

Then it dawned on me: Her husband's name was Brian too.

Lady Golfer

I was at the golf store comparing different kinds of golf balls. I was unhappy with the women's type I had been using. After browsing for several minutes, I was approached by one of the good-looking gentlemen who works at the store. He asked if he could help me.

Without thinking, I looked at him and said,

'I think I like playing with men's balls.'

Unofficial royal photographer

I had one hugely embarrassing moment when I approached a man whom I thought was a James Hewitt lookalike and asked him if he would appear in one of my photographs.

He replied, 'I actually am James Hewitt –

and I am afraid you cannot afford my fees.'

Nina Simone

A limousine had just pulled up to the backstage entrance of Ford Auditorium where Nina Simone would be performing in less than an hour.

The legendary, eclectic song stylist evidently had neglected to 'secure her assets', so to speak. She had what was later to be called a 'wardrobe malfunction'.

As she stepped out of the limo, one of those 'assets' popped out. Nina didn't miss a beat.

She pulled out the other 'asset', shook them at the crowd, popped them back where they belonged and, then, proceeded to make her grand entrance.

Diana Ross

Diana Ross was out and about with her children one day when a celebrity photographer (of the paparazzi variety) began taking pictures. Well, the super diva just wasn't having it that day.

**She took off her shoe
and chased the photographer.**

But she tripped and ended up sprawled on the ground, still with the shoe in her hand. The photographer stopped running, turned around and began taking pictures of that, and those are the pictures that a tabloid published.

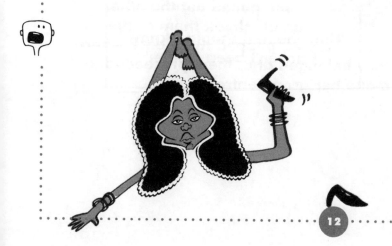

Emery King (Newscaster)

Emery King, Channel 4's outstanding veteran newsman, told the Chronicle that his most embarrassing professional moment came when he was working for a station in another city.

He was broadcasting live on the lawn of the White House and had apparently been there a long time, in the cold. Nerves were frayed. The reporter at the station, the one doing the newscast, asked King what was going on inside the White House.

Not realising he was on the air, an irritated King replied,

'How the hell should I know? I haven't been inside.'

Gwyneth Paltrow

I was wearing a pair of pink suede trousers at a premiere, and when I got up I thought something felt a bit wrong.

The whole crotch of my pants had split all the way up the back! Worse, I wasn't even wearing a thong.

There were reporters everywhere.

I just grabbed my pink pashmina and wrapped it around myself.

At the time, I was going out with Brad Pitt. Afterwards he said, 'We share the same bed and you don't even show me that much.' He loved to bring it up in company, and he was always delighted to tell them that I hadn't been wearing any knickers.

Alicia Keys

I was doing an schmoozy show, and it was going really well. Then suddenly, I took a spill and fell over a monitor. My mike hit the ground and it sounded like I cracked 25 teeth.

I thought, 'I can't believe I'm falling right now!'

Then I got up and the next number was, 'I keep on fallin'...'

Stupidly I sang it. Everybody laughed. I just grit my teeth and carried on. But the show was never going to come back from that... and it didn't.

Beverly Mitchell

I was talking to this guy whom I was totally into, and my friend thought she'd do me a favour; she pulled down my pants a little because they were too high on my waist.

Unfortunately, she completely pantsed me!

I WAS SO SHOCKED, I JUST STOOD THERE IN MY PANTIES AS IF NOTHING HAD HAPPENED.

Jessica Simpson

Pop princess Jessica Simpson and her husband Nick Lachey look like dumb and would-be wife-beater on their US reality show *Newlyweds*. **The 23-year-old blonde from Waco, Texas, didn't know buffalo wings were not made of buffalo.**

But she surpassed herself when she confused chicken with tuna. While holding a can of Chicken of the Sea, she asked Nick:

'Is this chicken what I have, or is this fish? I know it's tuna. But it says chicken. Is that stupid? Why is it called chicken of the sea?'

Lachey, 29, glared at her in utter amazement, and replied witheringly:

'A LOT OF PEOPLE EAT TUNA, A LOT OF PEOPLE EAT CHICKEN, SO IT'S LIKE CHICKEN OF THE SEA.'

Winona Ryder

Winona Ryder was caught shoplifting $5,500 worth of clothes from Saks Fifth Avenue in Beverly Hills, when Security guards stopped the 32-year-old star outside the store on December 13, 2001. The police charged her with theft.

Loaded down with bags, the Edward Scissorhands star had cut holes in some chic designer garments to remove security tags.

Humiliation was piled on shame when the store video of her modus operandi was shown all over the world.

The jury rejected her pleas of innocence and she convicted, then sentenced to 480 hours of community service, 3 years' probation, $10,000 in fines and restitution.

Afterwards a friend [!] said, 'Winona is frigid and the only way she can get her rocks off is stealing frocks.'

Jessica Simpson [Again]

When I went to the White House to meet the President, I was introduced to the Secretary of the Interior, Gale Norton.

I said, 'I really like what you've done with the place.'

I had no idea that she was a member of the Cabinet, not an interior decorator!'

Elizabeth Taylor

The 71-year-old actress learned the hard way at the Golden Globes in 2001 that it is customary to announce the nominees before announcing the winner.

Seemingly disoriented, Taylor was due to present the final award – Best Film Drama. But she almost gave away the surprise when she began to open the envelope in front of millions of viewers.

Host Dick Clark rushed on stage and told Liz to read from the autocue.

Looking like a deer caught in the headlights, Liz replied, 'What?' before realising her blunder. 'I'm sorry,' she said to the star-studded audience.

'I'm new at this!'

Ben Gallop
(Editor of Sport Interactive, BBC)

Like all journalists, I have fallen prey to the odd slip of the typewriter and produced something in print that I was be ashamed of. I can remember one time when Bradford City were promoted from the First Division to the Premiership and I was doing a match report on a particular game; a stunning goal went in and I reacted by writing

'and the goal set Valley Parade alight'.

Now I did this in all innocence, not realising until a few hours later, when we were inundated with emails, that Valley Parade, of course, was the scene of an horrendous tragedy about fifteen years ago, when a fire killed numerous people there. That was deeply embarrassing and something that I had to apologise for. So, we can all do it and but you just hope it doesn't happen too often.

Shirley Manson (Garbage vocalist)

I was onstage with a former band, and I went for a pee just before the gig. I ran to the toilet, ran onstage and did the show.

When I came offstage, I realised that the back of my skirt had been tucked into my knickers the entire gig. There were, like, 45 record company representatives in the audience.

Everybody had seen my ass! Which to be frank ain't that great.

It was awful.

Brad Pitt

Says his most embarrassing moment was discovering he had a spot on his bum during one particularly raunchy scene. It was covered up by a make-up girl... using a toothbrush!

He recalls:

'You're on a set and it's "Cut! Come here – you've got a zit on your butt."

'You're standing there and this make-up lady's putting pancake on your butt with a toothbrush.

'It made me laugh in a way. But what wasn't so funny was being told what she said when she walked off the set:

"I've seen hampsters with bigger dicks."

George Clooney

The actor George Clooney, who recently had to bow out of promotion work for his film *Ocean's Twelve* because he was suffering from a ruptured disc, is renowned for being touchy about his encroaching years.

The 43-year-old admits that some people think he's much older than that – and a joke about his age was even put into the film's script, after a real-life cringe encounter.

George revealed: I was in Italy last year and a younger girl said to me,

'Hey, Georgio. How old are you?'

I, stupidly enough, asked a question that you should never ask, which is,

'Well, how old you think I am?'

She answered, '50.'

I said raising my eyebrows, 'You think that I'm 50 years old?'

All this did was raise the ante

She suggested, '51?'

So Steven thought it would be funny to put it in the film. The bastard.

George Lopez (actor and comedian)

One time I was doing a show at this amphitheatre with about 6,500 people, and my fly was down.

During a lull, this guy in the front row shouted out,

'Hey, man, your zipper is down and there's a little winkle peeping out.'

Leslie Ash

When I was doing *The Tube*, I spent an entire interview referring to Robert Palmer as Robert Plant. I also announced that it was the anniversary of the death of Martha Luton King!

After that I just wanted the ground to open up and swallow me.

Girth Gurdler (Guitarist, Grand Cassa)

During a school assembly I described
Nepal as the team Maradona played for.
(Maradona's team was Naples)

Carol Smilie's cringe:

**Showing my post-childbirth stitches to
the hospital cleaner, assuming she was a
doctor.**

Zoe Lucker's cringe
(Actress)

Sitting on a train after filming one of
Tanya Turner's cocaine-snorting scenes in
Footballers' Wives.

**Two blokes were staring at me when I
scratched my nose – and loads of
glucose powder fell out.**

Of course, I made it worse by trying to explain that I was an actress... They ended up talking to me as if I should be booked into The Priory before the men in white coats carted me off.

Neil Jackson (Phil Wallis in *Dream Team*)

I used to box, and years back had a pro fight that was shown live on Channel four. I told all my mates to watch, my family came down to Cardiff for it, I even joked with Joe Calzaghe, who was ringside, to watch out as I'll be after his title next.
I got knocked out in the first round!

Serena Williams' cringe

'Just the other day, at a very big event, I had a very low dress on, and it, um... kind of fell!'

What Serena fails to mention is that some of the men who unwittingly witnessed the event are still suffering from post-traumatic shock. Serena should leave wardrobe malfunctions to her older sister, Venus (the pretty one).

Roselyn Sanchez (actress)

I was doing a film once. It was my first English job. I was supposed to cry, and we only had one take.

I was so nervous that if I didn't cry they would fire me.

I was backstage cutting onions but I STILL DIDN'T CRY!

Everybody was laughing at me. Then, I had to do the scene.

When it was my cue to cry, I started laughing hysterically.

They fired me, all right.

George Brown
(Labour Foreign Secretary 1966-68)

Response to a drunk George Brown at a diplomatic reception;

'I shall not dance with you for three reasons.

First because you are drunk,

second, because this is not a waltz but the Peruvian national anthem and, third,

because I am NOT a beautiful lady in red; I am the Cardinal Bishop of Lima!'

Earl of Oxford

In John Aubrey's *Brief Lives* is the story of the Earl of Oxford, who bowed deeply to the first Queen Elizabeth and accidentally farted.

Overcome with shame he vanished from court and spent seven years travelling.

On his hesitant return, the queen greeted him with:

'My Lord, I had forgot the Fart.'

Ambassador

The British ambassador to Mexico was asked by a local TV station what he would like for Christmas, after debating the ethics of such a gift with his questioner he decided upon a small box of crystallised fruits.

On Christmas day he was watching television when the newsreader announced, '...and finally, we asked the ambassadors to our country what they would like for Christmas.

The French ambassador said he wished for world peace, the Canadian, a cure for cancer and the British?'

A small box of CRYSTALLISED FRUITS.'

The Prince of Cringe

The prince dipped into the problems of joblessness at the height of the recession in 1981, grumbling:

'Everybody wanted more leisure. Now they complain they're unemployed.'

The prince insulted a group of deaf youngsters seated next to a loud steel band by saying:

'If you're near that music it's no wonder you are deaf.'

One of the most famous clangers was made during the 1986 state visit to China when he told British students:

'If you stay here much longer, you'll all be slitty-eyed.'

In the Cayman Islands in 1994 he asked a wealthy islander:

'Aren't most of you descended from pirates?'

In Australia in 1998 he suggested that tribes in Papua New Guinea were still cannibals.

'You managed not to get eaten, then?' he rhetorically asked a British student who had just trekked the Kokoda jungle trail.

After the Dunblane massacre in 1996, Tony Blair committed a future Labour Government to banning all handguns. When the proposed Bill was announced, after Labour gained office, Phillip pointed out:

'If a cricketer decided to go into school and batter people with a cricket bat, are you going to ban bats?'

Dunblaners were not amused.

He said to a British student in Hungary:

'You've not been here long, you haven't got a pot belly.'

38

To a bare breasted Masai lady presenting him with a gift:

'Err... you are a woman, aren't you?'

To a Scottish driving instructor, he commented:

'How do you keep the natives off the booze long enough for them to actually pass their test.'

Asian business leaders and councillors in Coventry hit out at the Duke of Edinburgh's observation that a tatty fuse box he saw looked like...

'... it was put in by an Indian.'

Tim Henman

Tim claims that his most embarrassing moment was the first time he made the headlines as a less than perfectly-behaved icon of middle England.

In a fit of temper during the 1995 Wimbledon doubles championships he smashed the ball into the back of the court, accidentally hitting it into ball girl Caroline Hall's face.

He later made it up with Caroline with a bunch of flowers and a big kiss.

The notoriously humourless Henman added deadpan:

'Lucy, my fiance at the time, accused me of being unfaithful!'

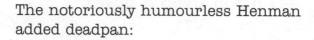

Kate Winslet

One embarrassing moment that I wouldn't mind deleting was...

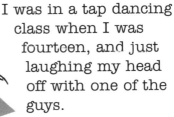

I was in a tap dancing class when I was fourteen, and just laughing my head off with one of the guys.

I don't know what we were laughing about. We just kind of got ourselves into that hysterical thing that you can't get out of.

And I actually peed myself in the class. So badly.

It was terrible. I never lived it down.

Geri Halliwell

SCOOP
the
POOP

Geri Halliwell and her pet shih-tzu,
Harry, once visited Tony Blair at Chequers
(the British Prime Minister's rural
residence). Geri was on her best
behaviour.

And Harry?

'We were in Mr Blair's study,' Geri later recalled, **'and Harry went into the corner of the room and defecated on a carpet!**

'I was so embarrassed;
**I had to ask for tissues
to clear it up...**'

Rene Zellweger

Horrifying love scenes. Horrifying.
They're so uncomfortable, and you know what?

It's funny 'cos I trust these guys completely and I know them well and I adore them and I have so much respect for them and they are my friends.

I've known them for a long time and still it's so awkward, you know, with the 200 people around and the blaring lights and you're trying to look into each other's eyes.

It's so awkward and you just want to get through it 'cos there is lots of giggling where it's not intended, and you just feel so stupid.

YOU ALSO KNOW THAT EVERY MAN – FRIEND OR WANNABE LOVER – IS LOOKING AT YOUR BOOBS AND NEVER MIND THE FILTHY THOUGHTS IS WONDERING IF THEY ARE SILICONE OR NOT.'

Billie Burke (Actress)

While she was enjoying a transatlantic ocean trip, Billie Burke, the famous actress, noticed that a gentleman at the next table was suffering from a bad cold.

'Are you uncomfortable?' she asked sympathetically. The man nodded.
'I'll tell you just what to do for it,' she offered. 'Go back to your stateroom and drink lots of orange juice. Take two aspirins. Cover yourself with all the blankets you can find. Sweat the cold out.

I know just what I'm talking about.
I'm Billie Burke from Hollywood.'

The man smiled warmly and introduced himself in return.

'Thanks,' he said,
'I'm Dr. Mayo from the Mayo clinic.'

Jennifer Aniston

That first year we shot to number one in summer reruns. People came over to me at a drugstore one day and said,

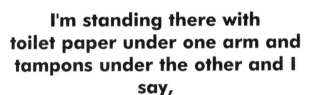

'We've been following you for blocks and just wanted to know if it was you, and could we have your autograph?'

I'm standing there with toilet paper under one arm and tampons under the other and I say,

'Sure.'

The trouble was as I went to sign my autograph the tampons dropped on the ground. This young man bend down, picked them up and said,

'ARE THESE YOURS?'

Leo F. Buscaglia (Author)

When speaking in public I perspire profusely, and thus always carry a few neatly pressed white handkerchiefs.

Once, before a large audience, I had already used two handkerchiefs.

I reached for number three and proceeded to wipe my forehead...

...only to find to my horror that I was using a pair of pressed white briefs, underwear that had inadvertently been piled among the handkerchiefs!

With as much poise as I could muster, I completed the dabbing and quickly returned the underwear to my pocket.

The embarrassment made me sweat all the more but I was terrified that if I took out another handkerchief, the same thing would happen...

I finished up looking like a boiled lobster.

Sir Thomas Beecham (Conductor)

Once saw a distinguished-looking woman in a hotel foyer. Believing he knew her, but unable to remember her name, he paused to talk with her.

As the two chatted, he vaguely recollected that she had a brother. Hoping for a clue, he asked how her brother was and whether he was still working at the same job.

**'Oh, he's very well,' she said.
'and still King.'**

Peter Rennie
(broadcaster Tauranga, New Zealand)

When her Majesty Queen Elizabeth visited New Zealand in the 1960s, it was my job as a broadcaster to give the live description of events. My vantage point was on the main street of a small town where the queen was scheduled to pass.

I carefully thought through my description of the scene, but my nervousness showed when I announced to the whole country,

'And here comes her Majesty now, **wearing a beautiful frummer sock!**'

The Duke of Edinburgh, standing next to me, made it worse. Deliberately, I'm sure.

His snort of derisory laughter was also broadcast to the nation.

Bishop

The wife of a retiring bishop was impressed when she and her husband left the home of their host, the Episcopal bishop of Panama, and found a crowd waiting near the front of the house.

Having seen these people during a morning church service, she greeted each one present and thanked them for such a warm good-by.

Her enthusiasm waned, however, when a city bus appeared and the puzzled crowd climbed aboard.

Jenna Jameson

After attending the Private Parts premiere in 1997, porn star Jenna Jameson went to a party with Goth rocker Marilyn Manson.

'On the way Manson took the opportunity to kiss me, I had a good buzz and thought "Bring it on."

'When we arrived at the party, everyone was looking at me funny.

'Soon after when I passed by a mirror I realised that I had his black lipstick all over my face.

 'I LOOKED LIKE I'D BEEN EATING MUD.'

Ronald Reagan

In 1984, at the height of the Cold War, he said: 'My fellow Americans, I am pleased to tell you I just signed legislation which outlaws Russia forever. The bombing begins in ten minutes.'

He was joking around in a voice-level test before broadcast, but it turned out the microphone was switched ON.

While making a toast to Princess Diana he called her **'Princess David'**.

Of Margaret Thatcher:
'She's the best man in England.'
No one was sure whether or not he meant it.

George W Bush

US President George Bush, famous for his verbal gaffes, once threw Japan's money market into panic.

After meeting Japanese premier Junichiro Koizumi in Tokyo, Bush said they had discussed **devaluation**. White House officials hastily briefed reporters that Bush had used the wrong word – he should have said

deflation

and elsewhere...

'This is Preservation Month. I appreciate preservation. It's what you do when you run for president. You gotta preserve' (remarks during 'Perseverance Month,' Los Angeles Times, Jan. 28, 2000).

'You teach a child to read, and he or her will be able to pass a literacy test.'

'I promise you I will listen to what has been said here, even though I wasn't here (Aug. 13, 2002).'

'I've coined new words, like misunderstanding and Hispanically' (March 29, 2001).

John F Kennedy

In June 1963, John F. Kennedy stood at the Berlin Wall and intoned, 'Ich bin ein Berliner,' which actually translates as...

'I AM A CREAM BUN.'

Al Gore (former US Vice President)

'It isn't pollution that's harming the environment.

It's the impurities in our air and water that are doing it.'

David Bowie

Rock legend David Bowie came on stage for a massive gig at Roker Park in Sunderland in 1987 and announced: **'Helloooo Newcastle!'**

Another one of David Bowie's most embarrassing moments was when he went to see Elvis Presley live.

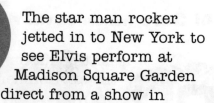

The star man rocker jetted in to New York to see Elvis perform at Madison Square Garden direct from a show in London in 1972 – but he arrived 10 minutes into a 45-minute appearance.

He says, **'I had the humiliating experience of walking down the centre aisle to my very good RCA-provided seat while Elvis performed 'Proud Mary'.**

'I was in full Ziggy Stardust regalia – brilliant red hair and Kabuki platform shoes.'

Shannen Doherty
(Actress, Beverly Hills 90210)

When Shannen Doherty did a Playboy photoshoot the guys were queuing up to see her naked. The pin-up insisted on a closed set for the shoot but soon realised her idea of privacy wasn't the same as the photographer's.

She remembers, 'We rented this house and all of a sudden the gardeners came and the guys that clean out the fish tanks came and then you have the owner of the house walking around.

'I'm really shy and all these guys are cruising around. But the worst moment was when this young girl arrived with an ice bucket and proceeded to rub both my nipples with an ice cube to make them erect.

'As she did it, the set went unnaturally quiet and I looked up and the men were drooling and looking at me with their eyeballs on stalks. **I knew, then, that not even money is compensation enough for doing some things.'**

Dave Gahan
(Musician, Depeche Mode)

Dave Gahan's most embarrassing moment ever was when a child asked him his name – and he couldn't remember it. The wildman rocker – who has a troubled history with drink and drugs – woke up on a friend's couch after a heavy night to be faced by the inquisitive tot.

Dave, 41, says, 'I arrived at my friend's house with no shirt or shoes on. She graciously let me stay on her couch. I was very drunk and had no idea where I'd left my shirt or shoes.

I came to on the sofa and a little kid was staring at me in the face asking me who I was, and all I remember is not being able to answer him. He then said, I am going to call the police. You're a burglar.' I told him that I was a friend of his mum's. The trouble was I held his arm as I did.

He screamed,
'Mummy, this man is touching me!/

Arnold Schwarzenegger
Governor of California

TERMINALLY
EMBARRASSING!

Adam Brody (Actor, The OC)

Adam experienced the awkward side of his fame, when he was pursued by a middle-aged woman in a supermarket. While the 26-year-old is enjoying the attention of his fans, having older admirers chase him in public is something that will take some time to get used to.

Brody says, 'I am always approached by people who recognise me. A lot of the teenage girls get so excited when they see me. They all want a hug, and you know, that's cool in a way.

'But recently, I was in this crowded supermarket and **this middle-aged woman came up to me, screaming my name, and wanted me to hug her.**

'That was really uncomfortable. Everyone was watching. I wanted to be polite, but it was embarrassing for me. The worst was she started squirming her crotch into mine.'

Sting

The rocker was left red-faced when he went hunting for his star on the Hollywood Walk of Fame after fans realised what he was doing.

The Brit, who was in Tinseltown preparing for a low-key club show at The Roxy took a bandmate for stroll along Hollywood Boulevard, where they tried to find his pavement star honour.

He says, 'We walked very very quietly, discreetly down the street and I couldn't see it.

**'I walked back a little way
and some guy said,**

"STING, YOUR STAR'S OVER THERE."

'He knew exactly what I was doing.'

Colin Farrell

Revisited his embarrassing past on comedienne Ellen DeGenere's daily chat show in America when he had to teach the host and three audience members linedancing moves.

The movie star used to teach country dancing in his native Ireland when he was a teenager, and Ellen insisted he gave a demonstration.

Embarrassed Farrell told her, 'There was a craze for a year when I was 17. This bird came in from Texas and taught us all how to linedance and then she went back to Texas and we linedanced and went around Ireland teaching people how to linedance.'

The Irishman was left red-faced when he tried to recall his skills.

He said, 'This is mortifying... We've had enough. I'm dying here, man.'

Earlier in the show, DeGeneres showed an early modelling picture of Farrell posing in a one-piece bathing suit, and she charged him $100 every time he swore.

It cost him $900.

CNN

Top news network CNN bosses blamed human error last year for leaking out mock-up pre-Easter obituaries for Paul Newman, the then Pope John Paul II and Fidel Castro among others.

The news service regularly updates obituaries in secret so they can be released immediately after a famous name passes away.

Kelly Hu (Actress, Xmen2)

When you're on a TV show or in the spotlight, you tend to be caught in a lot of moments. My first experience with that was with Miss Teen USA, and I was waiting at a bus stop and a guy came up to me and I thought he was going to ask me for an autograph. **But instead he told me that I had something on my nose!**

When I wiped it, I saw it was this monster booger. Sometimes God lays that stuff on you to bring you back to earth!

Kathy Rochford (News presenter BBC)

I was doing a vox pop of holidaymakers on a nudist beach near St Tropez when a respected, senior colleague from the BBC Birmingham newsroom tapped me on the shoulder.

I was wearing clothes but he wasn't...

I didn't know where to look! He laughed and said, 'If you look at him, he'll stand to attention.'

I was so embarrassed, I did look...

BBC

The BBC has said it is 'very embarrassed' after requesting an interview with the late music legend Bob Marley.

The request came in an email to the Marley Foundation asking the star to 'spend one or two days with us' for a documentary about his hit song 'No Woman, No Cry.'

In the letter, the BBC explained that filming was due to take place in the summer but added:

'OUR SCHEDULE IS FLEXIBLE.'

 Marley died of cancer in 1981 at the age of 36.

Brooke Shields

Smoking kills.

If you're killed,
you've lost a very
important part of
your life.

Alicia Silverstone

I think that *Clueless* was a very deep film.
I think it was deep in the
way that it was very
light.

I think lightness
has to come from a
very deep place if
it's true
lightness.

Andy Warhol

Dying is the most embarrassing thing that can ever happen to you, because someone's got to take care of all your details.

Stacey Farber (actress)

My friend lied to me and told me the stereo system in his car was voice-activated. I believed him and was yelling things like 'volume up', 'start' and 'eject' all night while he used a remote control. Needless to say, I was curled up when I found the remote.

Graham Norton (entertainer)

Interviewer: What was your most embarrassing moment?

Graham Norton:
Uhmm... lets start with prostitution!
(About his infamous rent boy career)

Michael Jackson/MTV

Michael Jackson had already spoiled one Brit award ceremony by pretending to be Christ, but our favourite MJ mishap came at 2002's MTV Video Music Awards.

Britney Spears welcomed the singer to the stage to accept a 44th birthday cake and described him as her 'artist of the millennium'.

Jacko took this to mean he was being honoured as the greatest singer of the last 1,000 years and gave an emotional acceptance speech **thanking God, his parents and, bizarrely, the magician David Blaine.**

Embarrassed MTV execs had to later explain that no such award existed.

Sinead O'Connor

The shaven-headed chanteuse appeared on America's Saturday Night Live in 1992 to perform songs from her latest album. For her second song however she chose a version of Bob Marley's War, which she brought to an end by shouting,

'Fight the real enemy!'

and ripping up a picture of the Pope.

Her performance was widely attacked, broadcasters NBC were fined $2.5 million and Frank Sinatra threatened to 'punch her in the mouth'.

O'Connor reluctantly disowned her performance, describing it as, 'a ridiculous act, the gesture of a girl rebel.' She provoked further criticism when she was later ordained as a priest.

Bob Dylan

If you're going to embarrass yourself, why not choose the biggest stage of them all? 1985's Live Aid was when stars on both sides of the Atlantic united to help the starving of Africa – shame no one told Bob Dylan though.

'It would be nice if some of this money went to American farmers,' he told a stunned audience.

Part of Africa's problem is the subsidies given to US producers, who then dump their surpluses on the third world.

Bob Geldoff commented 'It was a crass, stupid and nationalistic thing to say.'

Leonardo DiCaprio

Leonardo DiCaprio says he was left embarrassed in a supermarket when a woman complained about him without realising who he was. He said: 'I went to a supermarket with my cap and glasses on, and I was on the cover of a magazine.

'I was behind a woman at the checkout counter who was looking at magazines. She turned to me and goes,

"There he is again, that Leonardo DiCaprio. Don't you wish he'd just disappear?"

'I told myself that is the moment where I either go, "Do you know who I am?" or put my hat further down, pay for my CornNuts and get out of there.' I did the latter. As I went out I passed the same women. She shouted out,

"Bye-bye, Leonardo. Keep painting."

Brian Molko (Lead Singer, Placebo)

At an airport when we were flying to a festival in Sweden. We all got given our tickets and everybody disappeared to buy some duty-free. I noticed my flight was taking off an hour later than I thought. I was like, '**Oh my God, that's great, I've got loads of time**'.

After a while I started to notice there was nobody around any more, nobody I recognised. Then I realised I'd been looking at the Copenhagen flight which happened to depart one hour later, **I'd held up my own flight for 45 minutes.** There was Death In Vegas on board as well as several other bands. The captain was said,

'**Ladies and gentlemen, we're waiting for a certain Mr. Molko.**' When I finally walked on the plane, he added, '**Ahh, here he is.**' There was rapturous applause from all the passengers.

It was a long walk to my seat.

Jack Docherty (BAFTA awards host)

Almodovar's Best Director trophy marked a most embarrassing moment for host Jack Docherty, who said,

'And there's Pedro now going off to celebrate as the Spanish do, by chucking a donkey from a bell tower!'

Mark Blundell (Racing driver)

In 1992, I was the test driver for McLaren. We had a lot of fun during that year as well as hard work, and we were always clowning around. Since this was the last test, I'd had a bit of fun with the guys by swapping their hotel keycards so they were all locked out of their rooms. I'd also moved the entire contents of team manager Dave Ryan's room on to his balcony. I thought nobody knew it was me until the very end of my last test lap later that week.

**The minute I rolled into the garage, a
group of the guys had grabbed me in
the cockpit, tied my hands with tie-wraps
and swathed my head and torso in fairy
lights – like the ones you put on
Christmas trees.**

**Then they chucked a rope round my tied
wrists, put it through an eye hook in the
ceiling, unbuckled me and winched me
up there.**

**Then the fairy lights were turned on, I
had my helmet yanked off and they
smeared lipstick all over my lips and
cheeks.**

To add insult to injury, the garage door
was pulled open and I was left there for
about 10 minutes while a gang of press
photographers snapped away!

Photographs of that moment have been
doing the rounds ever since, and I cringe
whenever I see one. It's just lucky that it
happened at a test, not a Grand Prix. I'd
have died of shame!

Liv Tyler (actress)

Liv Tyler embarrassed herself when she undressed a doll based on her *Lord Of The Rings* character Arwen – then couldn't get its clothes back on. Liv got the doll from movie bosses, and couldn't resist checking its proportions against her own. She says, **'The boobs were pretty good – a lot bigger than mine.**

But then I couldn't get her clothes back on because her hands were too big. So I had to send her back in the box naked and I called to say,

'I'm really sorry, I'm not weird but I couldn't get her dress back on.'

Most Embarrassing Moments in BEATLES History

John Lennon's infamous 'Lost Weekend' hijinks, including slugging a waitress, heckling the Smothers Brothers and **sporting a tampon on his head**. (1974)

Paul McCartney being asked to open his suitcase at Narita Airport in Tokyo. Made all the more embarrassing because McCartney had been barred from entering Japan five years before because of his two previous marijuana arrests. (1980)
Paul and Linda McCartney being arrested for marijuana possession in Barbados almost four years to the day after the Japan arrest.

The embarrassment is compounded when they return to London, and Linda's suitcase is searched. **More marijuana is found, and she is arrested again.** The embarrassment is taken to dizzying heights when Paul blames the second arrest on Barbados customs officials for not searching Linda's bag thoroughly enough. (1984)

Ringo Starr appearing on 'The John Davidson Show' drunk and hostile. Low point: Davidson asking Starr what his favourite colour is (an asinine question, anyway) and Starr spitting back, **'I don't like brown!'** Davidson was dressed head-to-toe in brown. (1980)

The Paul McCartney song 'Bip Bop'. It's hard to believe this came from the same guy who wrote 'Hey Jude' just three years earlier. Even McCartney himself has disavowed it. (1971)

British Journalism

Jon Snow (Channel 4 News)

Jon Snow: 'In a sense, Deng Xiaoping's death was inevitable, wasn't it?'

Expert: 'Er, yes.'

John Humphrys

Doing the programme with a terrible hangover one morning and realising, half way through an interview with a leading politician, that I'd forgotten who he was.

And no, I'm not going to give you his name. I think he knows, but I'm not sure and I'VE ENOUGH ENEMIES IN WESTMINSTER AS IT IS.

John Sleightholme

As Phil De Glanville said, each game is unique, and this one is no different to any other.

Presenter (BBC Proms, Radio 3)

'Beethoven, Kurtag, Charles Ives, Debussy – five very different names.'

Presenter GLR

Presenter (to palaeontologist): 'So what would happen if you mated the woolly mammoth with, say, an elephant?'

Expert: 'Well in the same way that a horse and a donkey produce a mule, we'd get a sort of half-mammoth.'

Presenter: 'So it'd be like some sort of hairy gorilla?'

Expert: **'Er, well yes, but elephant-shaped, and with tusks.'**

LJo Whiley

When Radio 1 DJ recently underwent surgery she thought she was having a large mole cut off near one of her breasts, she was, however, shocked when her doctor told her it was actually a mini nipple!

She said: 'My husband has nicknamed me Scaramanga, after the James Bond baddie who also had three.'

Britney Spears

On what she does when she is upset: 'I always call my cousin because we're so close. **We're almost like sisters, and we're also close BECAUSE OUR MOMS ARE SISTERS.'**

Ben Stiller

I was in a band at high school and we gave a concert to some Jewish Association. We covered 'Hey, Jude.'

My father panicked, misunderstanding the lyrics. He started jumping up and down and waving his arms frantically, thinking **our lead singer was belting out 'Hey, Jew' to a roomful of Holocaust survivors.**

Christina Aguilera

I'm not really religious but very spiritual.
I give money to this company that
manufactures hearing aids on a regular
basis. More people should really hear me
sing.

I have a gift from God.

So, where's the Cannes
Film Festival being held
this year?

Marion Barry (Mayor Washington, DC)

Outside of the killings, Washington has one of the lowest crime rates in the country.

Jason Kidd
(Basket Ball Player, Dallas Mavericks)

We're going to turn this team around 360 degrees.

Danny Ozark
(American Football Coach)

**Half this game is
NINETY PER CENT MENTAL.**

Ashton Kutcher

I always used to get boners in science class; I don't know why. I'd try to hide them with my books. But one day this new girl sat next to me and noticed.

I was so embarrassed – she was obviously disgusted. But she hissed at me, 'Why don't you and your buddie do something about that.'

Advertising Gaffes

Vinnie Jones (footballer turned actor)

Gave a tough-guy performance in adverts for the alcoholic drink Bacardi Breezer. But the advert's screening coincided with his attacking a fellow passenger in an incident of air rage and he was, of course, **dropped from the campaign.**

Roy Keane

The fizzy drinks company 7-Up had Roy Keane as its figurehead in 2002, expecting him to be a World Cup hero.

But, as his face appeared on cans and advertising billboards, he flew home from the Far East after a massive fight with the Ireland team manager, Mick McCarthy, *before even kicking a ball.*

John Thompson (Comedian)

Appeared in ads for the banking giant Lloyds TSB just as he hit the headlines for **a series of alcohol-fuelled incidents in his private life.**

Sir Anthony Hopkins

Barclays bank used Sir Anthony Hopkins in 2000 to publicise the fact that it was a massive bank.

Unfortunately, as the campaign aired on television, the bank showed it was not so big-hearted by closing 171 branches, infuriating customers and staff alike.

Paul Kaye (Dennis Pennis)

Woolworth's picked the oddball comic actor Paul Kaye, of Dennis Pennis fame, to launch its Christmas campaign in 2002. **In interviews, he described himself in four-letter terms for doing the commercials and was subsequently dropped.**

David Beckham

Should have been a great choice for Brylcreem's target audience of young males –

except that after endorsing the product, HE SHAVED HIS HEAD!

Martin O'Neil
(Footballer turned Manager)

I was told to warm up at Clydebank and **I took my tracksuit bottoms off** and realised **I'd forgotten to put my shorts on.**

Charlotte Church

Introducing myself to and sitting down with three strangers in a Los Angeles hotel who I thought were writers I was due to have a meeting with.

I just started chatting away about myself and it wasn't until my mum arrived that I realised I was with the wrong people!

I wanted the ground to swallow me up!

Robbie Williams

I'm thinking of having a sex change.

I keep winning all the best male categories. It's getting boring now, so what I'm gonna do is just have the snip. Me and Alan Morissette **- she's gonna go male next year.**

Me mum tells this story about when I was three and we were on holiday in Spain and she lost me.

She was worried and went around the hotel looking for me. When she found me I'd entered myself into a competition.

I came onstage singing 'Summer Nights' from *Grease* as John Travolta. That's when she first realised that I was gonna do something.

After that I got a hat; I passed it around the pool and started singing for potato chips.

Brian Conley

It was getting recognised on a nudist beach in St Barts in the French Caribbean. I was letting it all hang out when a couple approached me for an autograph.

I love taking my clothes off. I'd do it a lot more if I wasn't famous.

Lucy Woodward (Actress, *EastEnders*)

Having an awful panic attack on the stage when I was doing a play must be my most embarrassing moment ever.

I can recall going through two hours of a performance not knowing any lines, although some words still managed to come out.

I then threw up during the interval and hyperventilated, and the whole room was spinning.

I think it was just because I was very tired at the time. I was filming in London and then commuting to Southampton to do this play. It was my first panic attack, so to have it happen on stage was very frightening.

Patrick Keilty

Hosting a live show from Belfast with guest Oliver Reed was quite embarrassing. To get the chat going I said:

'Welcome to Ireland, Ollie. How long have you lived here?'

Without a pause he replied: **'Young man, how long is your dick?'** Nuff said.

'Zoe Ball

I've done some very embarrassing things for love, but by far the worst involved actor Johnny Lee Miller.

I was in a bar when Johnny walked in. I'd just seen him in the film *Trainspotting* and had this big crush on him.

I was a bit tipsy, so I went up to him and started dragging him across the bar, shouting, 'YOU'RE LUVERLY.'

He disentangled himself and said icily, 'I am not *luverly* and you're definitely not sober.'

It was awful!'

James Martin (Chef, Ready Steady Cook)

I did a *Children In Need* telly show about three years ago with stars like Brian Turner, Antony Worrall-Thompson and Ainsley Harriott. We did a take on *The Full Monty* and stripped completely naked in front of about 15 million viewers and a lot more in the packed audience. Well, we had a little pouch on, but it left nothing to the imagination.

As the youngest and the newest on *Ready Steady Cook*, I drew the short straw and had to stand next to Ainsley.

That was my most embarrassing moment – I'll leave the rest for you to think about!

Tracy Shaw (Actress, Coronation Street)

The day I was doing a scene in the Rovers with Ashley.

We'd been filming for a while, then we were suddenly told to stop because my bra was showing and my boob was out!

I didn't even realise. There were red faces all round – but everyone had a good laugh at my expense… including me, until one of the crew said loud enough for me to hear, 'What she need a bra for?'

Tamzin Outhwaite (Actress, EastEnders)

I find it hard to live up to my glamorous screen image – in real life I'm a bit of a letdown.

Once I was in a hotel restaurant with a friend. I'd just had a shower and didn't have any make-up on. I noticed two girls at the next table and saw them nudge each other.

Then I overheard one of them say: 'I just don't understand what all the fuss is about. LOOK AT HER!'

Faye (Steps)

The most embarrassing memory I have is from my school days. I had a big crush on this one boy and during a PE session attempted to get his attention by doing a giant sneeze as he was about to do the high jump. The class had been told to be very quiet so he could concentrate but **my sneeze made him fall, and I got a week's detention.**

Samantha Robson (Actress, The Bill)

I was booked to appear on a music TV channel. They insisted I used their make-up artist. When she arrived she seemed a bit moody. I tried my best to cheer her up, but the more I tried the worse she got. I thought, 'Oh well, every one has their off days.'

But when she was finished I looked just like Dracula's daughter!

I was ushered onto the set, but I could see everyone was embarrassed for me. The director asked if I was happy with my look. Luckily, the make-up artist had gone for a break. So I was able to go the loo and start all over.

I made plenty of excuses for her, but she seemed to disappear. It's so embarrassing when you don't like someone's work.

How do you tell them?

Sally Lindsay
(Actress, Coronation Street)

I arrived at a club one night by cab and I remember seeing a bloke I really fancied. He was looking across at me, just sort of watching... but I couldn't work out why I was moving.

And then I realised what was going on – my skirt was caught in the door of the cab and it was driving off with me attached.

Eventually the inevitable happened – the skirt ripped, leaving me standing in the street in just my knickers.

He just stood there laughing at me, then he walked off as if I didn't exist.

I still cringe when I think about it.

Margi Clarke (Actress)

I started out as a presenter for *What's On*, on Granada TV. On one occasion for the show I had to go on a trampoline with a world expert.

I went and jumped about 30ft in the air – and promptly wet myself.

And once on the music magazine show *The Tube*, I fell over and did the splits, which I can tell you was as unintended as it was grossly embarrassing.

Terri Dwyer (Actress)

Things get no more embarrassing than falling off a catwalk, as I did once.

The catwalk was really thin and another model was not keeping to her side which made me fall off. To make matters worse, I was wearing a slinky long nightdress, which ended up over my head.

The trouble was the panty-line is taboo on the catwalk, so you do not wear knickers.

I scrambled back up on the stage and just carried on, which is all you can do in these situations.

Jessie Wallace (Actress, EastEnders)

I was playing Nell Gwynn in a stage play and in one scene I had to pull a coin out of my basque.
But just as I took it out, my boob came

out too! I had to think pretty quickly, so I just tucked it back in and carried on. I think I managed to save myself from being too embarrassed by trying to make it look as if it was just part of the drama, but everyone went a bit quiet when it happened – **well, they would, wouldn't they?**

Doon Mackichan (Comedian/Actress)

Weeing on stage after a giggling fit and having to go and change mid-scene and coming back in a pair of oversize chef's trousers.

Nell McAndrew

Having to go on my first weekend away (our first proper date) with my boyfriend Paul with an insect bite on my left cheek. I thought it was a spot and had tried to squeeze it, causing it to turn into a big, angry, scabby mess.

Noel Edmonds

When the Spice Girls appeared on House Party, I was taken behind the scenes and five people tore off all my clothes and put me in a mini skirt.

I was standing there starkers surrounded by young women! I've never been so embarrassed in my life.

Warren Clarke (Actor)

This guy broke into my car and I ran down the road after him in my dressing gown and slippers, waving an axe.

Unfortunately, somebody had called the police who came up to me and asked:

'Would you please not go around waving that axe or we'll have to arrest you.'

Antoine de Caune

I made a terrible mistake once when I was having dinner with some important people. I started saying nasty things about a woman who is a well-known writer and very respected. As I was talking, one of my friends was kicking my feet and I didn't know why.

Then this woman who was at the table said: 'That's my mother you are talking about.'

I was so embarrassed I wanted to die. I knew that there was nothing I could do to make it better – not even sending 2,000 roses would have made a difference.

Natalie Walters (Actress)

I once went out for a date with a bloke and spilt five glasses of red wine on his beautiful cream carpet.

The first time was embarrassing.

By the fifth I was mortified.

The trouble is, I get so nervous on a date that I shake uncontrollably. It didn't put him off though, as he asked me out the next week. The trouble is he stood me up and left me waiting in a bar

Weinermobile

One of my first jobs out of college was driving the Oscar Mayer Wienermobile. (And that's not the embarrassing part.)

One day, a co-worker and I were scheduled to bring the vehicle, which looks like a big hot dog on wheels, to a food show. As it always does, the car was attracting a lot of people. An elderly man approached and asked if it ran on mustard. I told him it didn't and even offered to give him a peek at the engine.

When he accepted, I made some comment like, **'Just don't scratch my buns,' and he laughed so hard his false teeth fell out –** **and got stuck in the Wienermobile's grill.**

With about 100 onlookers, I had to fish them out with a clothes hanger.

Break a leg?

After the birth of our third child, my husband and I decided that he should get a vasectomy. A couple days before the procedure, he hurt his leg doing yard-work and was walking with a limp. He had been told to have someone drive him to and from the vasectomy clinic where he was having his surgery. Since there was no one else available, I had to drive him and therefore take the kids with us.

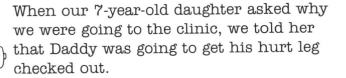

When our 7-year-old daughter asked why we were going to the clinic, we told her that Daddy was going to get his hurt leg checked out.

When my husband's surgery was done, he limped into the waiting room, which was filled with dozens of sombre men awaiting vasectomies.

Our daughter ran up to him and yelled, 'Daddy, Daddy, did they put a cast on it?'

Cut and Blow

I once walked into a hair salon with my husband and three kids in tow and asked loudly,

'How much do you charge for a shampoo and a blow job?'

Red Hot

My husband is a firefighter, and I am often at home alone and quite bored. One day, after experimenting with some new makeup, I thought I was looking pretty hot with nowhere to go. So I decided to take some pictures of myself using our computer's camera.

They weren't coming out as well as I'd hoped, so I made an onscreen 'video' of myself topless, which I then e-mailed to my husband for him to find when he came home and checked his e-mail account. It never occurred to me that he

might open it up from the computer at the fire station.

Sure enough, that evening I received a phone call from my husband, who was in hysterics because when he opened his e-mail at the station, **the video immediately downloaded and started playing on the screen, in front of his two firefighting buddies!**

Even worse, there was some sort of glitch on the computer and they couldn't close the video.

I'll never be able to show my face (or anything else) at the station again!

Gone to Pot

When my first child grew interested in the potty, I often found myself racing to take care of my business in the bathroom before she would inevitably come in and get in my way. So sometimes, I'd just scurry out of the bathroom without any pants on, just to get out of there as quickly as I could. One time I was walking around bottomless as my husband sat on the couch.

All of a sudden he screamed in horror at the top of his lungs:
'Ewww! There's toilet paper in your butt!'

I ran for the bathroom mirror and discovered that I had not wiped completely and was carrying a trail. I still haven't lived that one down.

The Law's an Ass

I once bought an Ally McBeal-like outfit: a slit-backed miniskirt and blazer. Like all my other clothes, the skirt fit too snugly around my hips and too loosely around my waist. But normally, this doesn't pose too much of a problem, so I wore my new ensemble to a job interview. The closest place to park once I got there was two blocks away from the office.

Unbeknownst to me, as I walked from my car to the building, my briefcase (which I was carrying at my side) slowly but surely hiked my skirt up around my body.

By the time I shook hands with the person I hoped would be my future boss, my skirt had completely turned around – with the sexy slit pointing straight to my... well, you can imagine.

All I could wonder was how many men out on the street had gotten a free stripshow.

Take Note

An insurance man visited me at home to talk about our mortgage insurance. He was throwing a lot of facts and figures at me, and I wanted to follow as best I could, so I told my 6-year-old son to run and get me a pad.

He came back and handed me a Kotex right in front of our guest.

Clinical Finish

I was at the health clinic and was told by the nurse to go into an examining room, take off all my clothes, and put on a paper gown.

After a few minutes, a man wearing surgical scrubs walked in. I jumped up, swung around, and asked him to tie the back of my robe because my butt was hanging out.

He obliged, then I hopped up on the table and asked what my test results were.

He said, 'I don't know. I'll get the doctor.'

It turned out that the maintenance workers there wore scrubs, too. When I walked past him on my way out, he grinned and waved good-bye.

Vehicle Reversing

I was standing at the checkout with my two-year-old son, and there was a heavyset gal in line ahead of us. As the cashier scanned the lady's items, the bar-code reader gave off a continuous beeping sound.

**All of a sudden, my son said loudly,
'Mommy, watch out!
She's going to back up!'**

That was one of the times in my life I wanted to crawl into a hole.

I know where the cops hang out

I'm a police officer, and one night while I was out on patrol, a description of a vehicle that had just been involved in a robbery came over the radio. Soon after, I saw a car that matched the description perfectly. I pulled the vehicle over, approached it with my partner, and spotted a gun under the passenger seat.

We got the suspects out of the car and onto the ground. **Just as I was pulling out the handcuffs, a loud noise that sounded like a digestive explosion ripped through the night. Then I felt a draft.**

Slowly it dawned on me that my pants had split from my crotch all the way up to my waist. I was standing frozen over the suspect, not sure what to do.

So I called my partner over and had him handcuff my suspect as I backed away to the cover of my patrol car. Imagine the holding-cell conversation that night about the female cop who had really bad gas!

Talking out of your...

I was dating two men, Les and James, and neither guy knew about the other. While romping around in bed one evening, Les grabbed my eyeliner pencil and scribbled 'I love Sandy' on my backside.

I forgot all about it. The next day, James invited me to a private pajama party at his house. You guessed it!

I'm lying stomach-down on his bed, and he says, 'Whoa, what's this on your butt?' I had a bit of explaining to do!

Aeroplane Loo

I was once on a flight from Auckland,
New Zealand to a small town way down
on the extreme souther tip of the South
Island called Invercargill.

The plane I was flying in was very old
propeller driven thing, I think it was a
C47 Goonie Bird.

The toilet was certainly not designed for a
guy my size because the bowl was against
the far wall, but the ceiling curved
backwards. I found myself leaning way
back like I was doing the limbo and trying
to urinate at the same time.

Being a propeller driven plane, we hit a
bit of turbulence. Because I was leaning
backwards so much, put my left hand
behind me to brace myself against the
door and continued to urinate.

My left hand accidentally hit the door
latch and I fell backwards into the aisle
and every passenger turned around to see

me laying in the aisle with my penis in my hand and I could not stop urinating for the life of me.

I got back into the toilet and composed myself. After another ten minutes, I returned to my seat and everyone started to applaud.

One old man thanked me for the funniest sight he had seen in all of his life. I have never returned to New Zealand since.

Dirty Underwear

I was nursing a nasty stomach bug when the guy I had wanted to date for a very long time asked me out. I decided to go ahead and go out with him even though I had been sick.

The big date came and I was feeling a lot better, though I still had some gas and whatnot. We went out to a nice restaurant and had a wonderful dinner. Then we went back to his place.

Everything was going splendidly. We were watching TV and fooling around when he got up to go pour us a glass of wine. I had been feeling a strong urge to pass wind since dinner and I figured that now would be a prime opportunity.

So I let her rip but something else besides the fart came out. I felt a wet sensation in my pants and I knew immediately that I has shit my pants.

I ran to the bathroom and took off my panties. I washed them with soap and water and buried my soiled underwear in the bottom of the trashcan underneath some papers.

I returned to the living room, where my date was waiting with glasses of wine. We started fooling around some more and just when things were getting heavy, his Yorkie, Sam, jumped right on top of us.

We both smelled a foul odour and I looked up to find Sam had something in his mouth. It had to be...

It was my dirty undies!
Mortified, I grabbed my purse, ran out the door, ran three blocks from his house and called a cab to pick me up.

At The Pool

Puberty can be a very cruel period for young pre-teens as it is, well have I got one for you.

Around the young age of 12 when the hormones just start kicking in and young boys discover young girls life can be interesting. During the dog days of summer the only way to really cool off is at the community pool. It was a summer ritual, a rite of passage a place where boys came of age during the summer

Well on one particular summer day the pool had a delayed opening so a rather large gathering formed outside waiting to get in. I would estimate about 20-40 kids, teenagers and a few adults. Me and my friends noticed a group of young girls about our age looking at us, I was sitting on the curb directly in front of them. One of the real cute ones stepped away from the other girls and came in my direction, yep she was checking me out, I was nudging my friends, suddenly my ego was sky high!!

I was like 'this is it!'

I am Charlie Brown and the cute red hair girl is going to dance with me. Oh I was feeling good as I watched her cross the street in my direction, smiling, what a beautiful face.....

Then it all came crashing down, in the middle of the street, she said and rather loudly I might add. 'Hey boy!' I looked up and smiled look at my friends like see I told you! She said again even louder: 'Hey boy!'

Now everyone is looking...

'Hey boy, your balls are hanging out.'

I look down at my swim trunks and sure nuff there they were, exposed for all to see. Everyone bust out laughing (my so-called friends, laughed the loudest) I was humiliated, left the area and went back home only to return to that pool days later. Even then some of the lifeguards would tease me about it.

If You Go Down To The Woods

Once when I was out hiking in the woods with my family, I desperately needed to pee.

But there were no toilets handy, so I wandered off the track a little way to select a suitable spot. I soon found a handy little spot, at the edge of a steep bank with a conveniently located handrail.

So I pulled my shorts and panties down to my ankles and squatted down, extending my bottom over the edge of the walk so I would not wet my shorts, and proceeded to pee, facing the area where I knew my family to be.

To my horror, as I was midstream, I heard a loud cheer behind me and turned slightly to see that a crowd of young men were observing me from the bottom of the bank.

The worst thing was that I couldn't stop and had to continue in that pose for about 30 seconds (which seemed like ten minutes) until I had finished.

All I could do then was to stand up, take a bow and make a speedy exit.

Booger

One day I was in class talking to this guy I had the hugest crush on. He told me how he was beginning to fall for me and asked if maybe we could go out.

In the middle of my answer I sneezed. I excused myself and told him that sure, I'd go out with him. He told me that he just remembered his parents didn't let him date and walked to the other side of the class.

I turned to my friend and asked what I did wrong and she said, 'Go look in the mirror, you've got a huge booger on your face!'

I pulled out my compact and sure enough a huge booger trailing snot had flew onto my cheek after I had sneezed. I couldn't look at that ex-crush for the rest of the year!

Pubic Hair

One summer when I was in college, my parents rented a lake cottage and invited a bunch of people – me, my two brothers, my mother's parents, and a guy they were trying to fix me up with.

I didn't plan on swimming, but my mom brought an old bathing suit and talked me into putting it on. I couldn't see well in the shower cabin, and it felt OK but a bit tight. When I walked back to the others, that guy stared right at my crotch! Everyone else looked embarrassed. I turned to him and said,

'What are you looking at, pervert?'

My mom rushed up and wrapped a towel around my waist. She told me to go in the house and look in the mirror.

When I got to a mirror, I could have died! There was half an inch of black short-and-curlies sticking out from each side of my bathing suit. I could hardly stand to look at anyone after that. Worst of all, my parents made me apologise for calling the guy a pervert.

Be All You Can Be

When I went to join the Army we were sent to Los Angeles to take our physical exam. There were about 50 in our group (clad only in our undershorts) and a rumour was circulating that we would go into one room and get a rectal exam.

Midway through the process we were all ushered into a room where a doctor was putting on rubber surgical gloves.

I knew this was it. We were all told to turn around, face the wall and drop our shorts. Now I was sure this was it!

The doctor came up behind me first. I felt a tapping on my back so I obediently bent over and 'spread my cheeks' for the dreaded rectal exam.

I heard the doctor say, 'What the hell are you doing?'

I looked back, as did 49 other recruits, to see the doctor standing behind me with a stethoscope!

All You Can Eat Puker

In the first few months of dating I was doing my darndest to make a good impression on this guy. He was a little wild, but I tried to keep up. I'd dieted myself down to a size five, never let him see me without make up, ect...

One afternoon, after drinking rum with him all night, he took me on the back of his motor cycle (and I hate motor cycles) to an all-you-can-eat buffet.

I had been on a diet for weeks so I splurged and ate three plates of food.

After finishing the meal, while chewing on some ice he told a joke and made me laugh. I choked on the ice and started coughing.

**I proceeded to puke. Not just a little...
I couldn't stop.**

I ran to the rest room puking all down my front and leaving a trail behind me. I was completely covered and told some lady in the bathroom to find him and tell him to go home without me.

There was no way I was going to wrap my arms around him to ride home. I walked, covered in my own vomit nearly a mile back to his house and sheepishly asked to use his shower.

Luckily, he was more worried than disgusted. That was four years ago and we are still together. (What a forgiving guy!)

Bad Vibes

My boyfriend bought me a vibrator for Valentine's Day about a year ago. Still living at home I knew I had to hide it. Well, after having some fun one night I just put it under my mattress.

The next day my little brother came in and laid on my bed, when he put pressure on the mattress, my vibrator turned on and started to buzz like crazy.

Well, not knowing what it was he came in the living room and said, 'sissy this was buzzing under your bed' and handed it to me.

It was a monday, so my mom and dad and I were watching *Fear Factor*, and looking at the size of my vibrator, my mom laughed and said, **'Apparently fear is not a factor for you.'**

And now my dad goes around saying, **'BZZZZZZZZZZ.'** I have never been more embarrassed in my life.

Co-Ed Dorm

During my first year in college, I lived on
the campus' first 'co-ed by room'
dormitory floor.

All the other floors had girls in one wing,
and boys in the other wing, separated by
a big shared lounge. But on our floor we
had girls next door and directly across
the hallway. It worked out great, and
there were no problems or complaints.

Anyway, one morning I woke up early
and had to take a leak, so I sleepily
shuffled down the hallway toward the
bathroom, wearing only my boxer shorts.
Nothing out of the ordinary.

I passed a couple of girls on their way to
breakfast and I mumbled a half-awake,
'Good morning.' They didn't respond.
Instead, they stopped walking, turned
around and watched me, as I walked past
them. Then they burst out laughing.

I thought, 'What's up with them?! This is
how people look in the morning, when

they're half awake.' I walked into the bathroom, stepped into the stall, and reached down to free the Big Guy for a much needed pee.

To my horror, the Big Guy was already out of the front of my boxes! And he wasn't looking the least bit sleepy!

He'd been proudly saluting all the way to the bathroom!

I guess it's true what they say: You can't keep a good man down.

Stamp Of Approval

I carry everything in my purse from stamps to tissues. Well I was going to the gynaecologist one day and I had to go to the bathroom for a pee. So before my appointment I went to the washroom, I did my business and then realised that there was no toilet paper in the bathroom. Being the resourceful woman I am, I reached into my purse and got a tissue and wiped myself.

Well, when I was being examined by the gyro, he started to laugh. I got a little offended and asked him what the hell was so funny.

He just looked at me trying to keep a straight face **and pulled a stamp out of my crotch!**

I guess what had happened was a stamp was stuck to the tissue I wiped myself with in the bathroom. From then on I kept my stamps and tissues separate to avoid this situation again.

Bed & Breakfast

My most embarrassing moment happened when I was staying at a bed and breakfast in Blackpool with three of my girlfriends for my 22nd birthday. We were in one of those cheap B&B (£15.00 per night) where we have to share a shower with the other guests.

We were all really looking forward to going out on the town that night and couldn't wait to get on our new clothes we brought. I gathered my towel and shampoo etc. and walked to the other end of the corridor, just after the stairs, to take a shower.

When I had finished, I gathered my dirty clothes and realised I had completely forgotten my clean ones. I had no intention of putting the dirty ones back on, so hoping no one was around, I attempted to run across the hall to our room with just my towel wrapped around me.

I opened the door and began to run for it, when a bloke came running up the stairs.

In and effort to cover myself up, my towel falls to the floor, leaving me completely naked.

That's not the worst of it. The next day during breakfast I had to sit almost opposite him, knowing what he had seen. My friends, natch, found the whole thing extremely funny.

Bicycle Shorts

I was once cycling on one afternoon in just my cycling shorts when suddenly without realising I skidded and fell.

As I hit the ground my shorts got caught in the cycle's chain and tore them right open. I was lying buck naked in the middle of the street with just my t-shirt to cover up my privates.

What made it worse was all the people who rushed over to see if I was hurt!

Blowfish

My Senior year in High school I met this great guy, and we had a habit of blowing into each others mouths when we were kissing. I always used to surprise him. Well, one day he surprised me and blew into my mouth.

He blew so hard that I wound up blowing snot all over his face.

I was mortified. (By the way, we didn't break up we got married!)

Dummy

I worked for a clothing company, and we had a full-size mannequin in our office. I used to cycle home after work, and was usually the last person in the office. One evening, I was changing into my cycle gear when a co-worker came back into the office. I immediately thrust myself behind the mannequin. My colleague took one look at me, formed the wrong conclusion, and left.

I updated my résumé the next day.

Digits

I was working in a small office opposite a very uptight lady. I was adding some figures on my desktop calculator, and as I got up to go to lunch, it slid off the file it was resting on and faced her desk, upside-down. Sadly, the number on it was **0.8537.** When I got back from lunch, she was threatening to sue me. She thought I was calling her a **LESBO!**

Gas Panic

I was interviewing for managers position with a company I had long wished to join. As the interview which had gone really well concluded I stood up and reached forward across the desk to shake the hands of the 5 people who had interviewed me, **and knocked over a glass pitcher drenching two of them!** To make matters worse at the same time I passed wind loudly... the odour was pretty bad . I was very embarrassed and, not surprisingly, did not get the job.

Fortune favours the brave

Giving a presentation to the executives of a Fortune top ten company to sell outsourcing and seeing that the word 'headcount' was missing the 'o' in every single slide where it was used. And then watching one of my team pronounce it the way it was misspelled!

Mr Soft

I opened the door to the conference room and leaned inside the door to relay a message to my boss. Little did I know that one of the male attorney had walked up behind me and was waiting for me to finish my conversation and move out of the doorway.

When I finished the message and while still facing forward, I reached my hand around behind me for the door knob and grabbed the attorney in the genitals instead.

I knew something was wrong immediately because the doorknob was 'soft' although round.

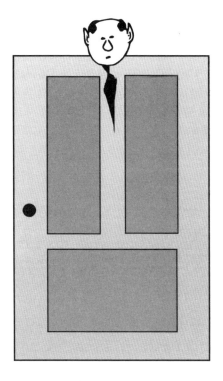

I could not look him in the face after that.

ATM

I work in a rather large consumer goods firm (approx 2000 people at our one location). I needed some cash one day so I walked down to our company ATM machine to make a withdrawal. As I approached the machine, I noticed a good friend of mine who worked in a totally different wing of the building. I glanced around, saw no one about, approached him, grabbed his ass squeezing tightly and said,

'Hey baby, I'd like to withdraw you.'

Imagine my dismay when he turned around and was NOT my friend, but a high level manager from another department! Conservative family man at that! I made my mortified explanation and apologies, then raced back to hide in my cubicle. From then on every time I ran into him in the hall, elevator, etc.,

I would turn bright red. I was SO happy when I was given the opportunity to move to a new company location!

Tissue

On my way to the first important job interview, my old car started to leak on my wing tip shoes. I grabbed some 'Kleenex' tissue and wedged some in my laces. After the interview and a long tour of the plant where I was introduced to dozens of people, I exited. The security guard said 'Hey buddy! What's all that toilet paper stuck in your shoes for?' I can't imagine what people thought – to their credit (I got the job) it was never mentioned to me during 6 years of employment there! How kind, yet how embarrassing.

Lab

Well I was in the lab getting ready to work and a college student, who was doing an internship from a women's college, poked me in the butt hitting my wallet.

Then she asked,
'What is that hard thing
in your pants?'

Big Bad John

I took a phone call from someone who said he was Jon and told me that the slide projector wouldn't work. Assuming it was Jon the summer intern I slowly and in a tone like I was talking to a three year old, I asked him if the machine was plugged in.

Then I realised that the John who had called me was the CEO of the corporation!

Hard Wire

I was giving a tour of my office's wiring closets to some potential business partners. When I unlocked the second closet, we were greeted with the site of one of our techies facing us – pants open, and getting intimate with himself, holding a rather saucy Men's Magazine.

First real 'wanker' I ever fired.

Holy Smoke

I worked in an office that was a townhouse. This was during the time that you could smoke in offices. So I went to make coffee in the kitchen and come back and ask my co-worker if she had a cigarette burning in the ashtray as I smelled smoke. She said no. I asked another co-worker if there were fire engines outside and she said no. I told them both I smelled smoke.

At that point I looked down and realised that I had singed my tie when I bent over to put the coffee pot on the stove. And it was still smouldering.

At least I then knew where the smoke was coming from.

Fur Factor

I was younger and working in the city, among an office of some 80 'would-be' executive types. Although we were friendly with one another, it was a competitive environment, and individually we all tried to look the part of the next to be promoted.
One weekend, while shopping in the thrift stores, I came across a used fur coat. It was priced very cheaply, only $10 less than the price of a couple of drinks, so I bought the coat, pleased to have acquired a luxurious garment at such an incredibly low price.

The following Monday was cold and snowing, and I was thrilled to be able to wear my 'new' fur coat to work and impress my colleagues and supervisors. Once at the office, I asked the supervising director – whose office was a glass-walled cubicle open to the rest of us on the work floor – if I could hang my coat in his office, on his coat rack.

All day, there on his coat rack, sat my wonderful fur coat, for all in the office to admire and envy, hung my fur coat.

At the end of the day, my supervising director came out of his office with my coat draped over his arm. Very gallantly he handed it over to me – or rather, held it up for me to put on – and as he was holding it, the fur literally fell apart in his hands, splitting seams and tearing until half of the coat fell to the floor, and the remaining half hung in his hands.

What I had failed to realise, knowing nothing about fur coats, was that old fur gets dried and and brittle, and can split at the slightest touch.

So much for my attempt at trying to impress others!

Trip

I went on a business trip with a good-looking, older but married guy. We got along, but were just friends. However, since I was a blonde in my twenties, his wife was not happy. Still, he talked about his wife and their wonderful, romantic trip there (to San Francisco) the whole time. At the next office get together, his wife cornered me and gave me the third degree. Trying to articulate that her husband was loyal to her, I said he talked about you and your wonderful trip there the whole time. His wife replied, 'That was his first wife.'

Oops!

Warm Reception

I was the receptionist at a very conservative law firm. One day one of the partner's wives came by for a surprise birthday party. She had a cake and some balloons. I buzzed the boss office but there was no reply. I thought he might have slipped out for lunch. We decided to bring everything back to his office and that way she could surprise him when he got back. When we opened the door we were amazed and surprised to find him in a compromising position with another woman straddling him.

He leaped up. The girl fell and hit her head on the desk on the way down. The cake went flying and hit him.

As she was running out of the office he went to run after her but he tripped on his pants which were still down around his ankles. He had screamed out

'It's not what you think!'

Needless to say I was asked to leave the firm but was given an excellent severance package and glowing references in return for my silence.

Heart Shaped Box

One Valentine's Day, I decided to shave my pubic area, paint a big red heart in lipstick down there, and present myself to my husband – stark naked – at the front door when he arrived home from work. When I heard the car pull up, I posed very seductively in front of the door and swung it open.

There stood my husband...
and his BOSS.

Say it with flowers

A few months ago, I was hopelessly infatuated with a man I work with. When I finally decided to express my affection for him, I chose the wimp's way out: I bought a single red rose and planned to put it in his car with a note during lunch.

But when I went to open the car door, the alarm went off.

The police arrived, and my secret crush came running to see what was going on. **There I stood like a total idiot, with the rose in my hand.** I gave it to him, and he read the card, smiled, and told the police it was a false alarm.

We've been dating ever since.

Spell Check

As a new manager, I thought it my duty to warn my staff that a recent increase in orders meant that we would have to work in two different shifts to get the orders processed in time. I sent a short email stating that 'shift work' was coming, and that they could expect a lot of 'shift work' in the next few months.

You know, if you leave the 'f' out of 'shift', the spell check won't catch it.

They still remember that email....

For Art's Sake

I am a 'Yank' who had an incredible
opportunity to work briefly for a firm in
London that managed fine arts. One day I
was entering information into the
database about some new works that
arrived in our warehouse. As it happens,
most of the art I was dealing with were
works by the 'YBA' (the Young British
Artists – Damien Hirst, Jake and Dinos
Chapman, Tracey Emin et.al.).

There is a work by Ms. Emin simply
entitled, 'My Big Fat Minge.'

Not knowing that 'minge' is a euphemism
for... ermmm... a part of the female
anatomy, I yelled out in my typical loud-
mouthed American fashion,

'What's a minge?'

No one answered. Everyone seemed to be
looking at their screens so intently that
they couldn't hear what I had said.

Ray W*******, actor

A few years back I worked on a movie that involved me spending a lot of time in Moscow. One evening a few us went to a nightclub called Nightflight. The place was stocked out with what Muscovites call 'butterflies of the night' – hookers. But English speaking ones as the place caters to a lot Americans and Brits.

I went to there to relax not pick up a girl... naturally. Inevitably, though, I did spoke to some – the crew invited them onto our table. One turned out to be a bit of a film buff and I talked to her for a bit. Russian with some Japanese in her – she black-haired, slight, not at what you'd reckon a hooker would like... very elegant and graceful. Her name was Alexandra.

But there it stopped...well, that night. However, we did meet again and we started seeing each other, not as hooker and client but like any couple.

Whenever I flew back to London I would

see my wife and children but we were no longer an item. Meanwhile, back in Moscow, I moved in with Alexandra and I did pay for her flat but that was the only money that I gave her

I didn't tell anyone except my mother that I was seeing someone. And her, I just said I was going out with a Russian actress.

For a few months things were okay but Alexandra started getting jealous over my seeing my wife when I went to London. What happened was she went through the call history on my mobile while I was asleep, and discovered I'd been calling Tina.

She decided she'd call my mother whose number she got from my mobile, too.

She got through to Mum and introduced herself as my girlfriend in Moscow. Of course, Mum said that I had told her about her but Alexandra assumed that I had gone into details. She didn't know

that I had told Mum she was an actress. Anyway, she was upset about the possibility of my going back to my wife, so she wasn't thinking too clearly.

She was going on about how she knew that I was ringing my wife and seeing her when I was in London. My mother assured her that the marriage was over and this was to do with the children.

Alexandra then told her, 'I want you to know that I love your son so much I have not slept with a man for money for four months.'

My mother couldn't believe her ears but she asked how she lived and Alexander answered, 'Ray gives me money.'

I knew nothing of all this as Alexander said nothing, and my mother was too shocked to mention it. However, she did tell my wife.

When I next went to London, they were both waiting for me. It was obvious something was wrong. Tina said, 'You didn't tell me that you were seeing a Russian actress while you were in Moscow.' I just mumbled something about not having to ask her permission to see someone.

Then, with my mother looking on all shame-faced, she said, 'Well, she rang Mum.

'You're a liar – she's a prostitute and you're paying her for sex. How disgusting. What will the children think?'

I couldn't speak. I just wanted to the earth to open up and take me down to hell... where I think I'd have felt more comfortable.